board sports

Isabel Thomas

First published in 2011 by Wayland

Copyright © Wayland 2011

Wayland
Hachette Children's Books
338 Euston Road
London NW1 3BH

Wayland Australia
Level 17/207 Kent Street
Sydney NSW 2000

Concept by Joyce Bentley

Commissioned by Debbie Foy and Rasha Elsaeed

Produced for Wayland by Calcium
Designer: Paul Myerscough
Editor: Sarah Eason

Photographer: Adam Lawrence

British Library Cataloguing in Publication Data

Thomas, Isabel, 1980–
    Board sports. — (Street sports)(Radar)
    1. Skateboarding—Juvenile literature.
    I. Title II. Series
    796.2'2-dc22

ISBN: 978 0 7502 6459 4

Printed in China

Wayland is a division of Hachette Children's Books, an Hachette UK company.

www.hachette.co.uk

Acknowledgements: Alamy: PCN Chrome 8–9; Doomwheels 25r; Flickr: Sharese Ann Frederick 2bg, 21tl; Getty: Darryl Leniuk 25l, Wireimage 2cl, 10; Nancy NG Photography 2tc, 12–13; Rubicon: Lotta Anulf 28–29, Tim Parker 22; Shutterstock: Afaizal 3br, 20bl, Magnum Johansson 30–31, Andrey Khrolenok 24bl, Ronen 1, 4–5.

cover stories

12

FEEL IT
Read all about the buzz of mountainboarding!

10

STAR STORY
Find out about the life of skat...

6

INTERVIEW
...d skateboard ...ends us his ...ise!

GET THE GEAR
Find out what *you* need to start boarding

thepeople

themoves

thetalk

LOVE & SKATE!

Take a wooden board, add four wheels, and you have a passport to an insane number of ways to have fun. From adrenalin-fuelled racing and breathtaking tricks to jamming with friends, board sports have it all. Here are the wheel-based sports that are leading the boarding revolution…

SKATEBOARDING TAKES OFF

In the 1940s, surfers began riding boards with wheels and created the world's most popular extreme sport. From street to skate park, there are many different styles of skateboarding. Flatland skaters pull tricks on flat ground, while vert skateboarders use ramps to grab big air and perform spectacular aerial stunts.

SPEED ON WHEELS

In a quest for more speed, some skateboarders in the 1960s made their own boards by fixing wheels to surfboards. These became known as longboards. These new boards were longer, faster and better at turning than regular skateboards. Longboarding soon became a sport on its own, with special boards and a new range of skills to master. Longboards are used for downhill and slalom racing, or just cruising the streets for fun.

Type 'land kiteboarding' into www.youtube.com to see this amazing board sport!

KITEBOARD CRAZY

Land kiteboarders use a kite and the wind to pull them along flat terrain at speed. Riders can grab amazing air, so they have their feet strapped to the board ready to do flips and tricks. Many land kiteboarders ride on beaches, but a field or football pitch on a windy day are as good.

MOUNTAIN MAYHEM

Mountainboarding is like snowboarding but without the snow! Sturdy boards with inflatable tyres are used for downhill riding, dirt track racing and freestyle stunts. Freeriding mountainboarders launch themselves down all kinds of terrain just for the challenge.

GEOFF ELSE

Radar expert Geoff Else has been skating since he was 14 and now runs a top UK skate school. Radar talks to Geoff to find out what he loves about skating and to steal his secrets for getting into the board sports scene...

What do you love about skateboarding?

It's challenging and has a different philosophy from other sports. Even if someone is beating you in a competition, you'll still be stoked and cheering them on. There is a special connection between skaters – how can you top that?

6

Have you ever had any serious wipeouts?

I've broken each wrist four times, broken my ankle and dislocated my arm. The list goes on! Skating can be brutal, but a little common sense makes it much safer.

How did you get into the skate scene?

I was hooked the moment I saw my brother's mates doing slides and flips on home-made ramps. I pestered my dad to get me a board and I haven't stopped skating since!

What kind of board is best for beginners?

You don't need to splash out on a pro skateboard on day one, but do avoid the kids' boards that are sold in toyshops. Visit a specialist skate shop and choose a board that's safe and will last a long time.

What are your top skateboarding tips?

Always wear full protective gear, including a helmet, elbow pads and knee pads. Try to push yourself to achieve bigger and better stunts, but only within your comfort zone – never try anything too soon. Also never feel pressurised by anyone to try something you're not comfortable doing. That's the beauty of boarding – you can take it at your own pace!

Any other tips for beginner skateboarders?

Warm up and stretch before a big session. Don't skate when you're tired or push yourself beyond your limits. (But do push yourself a little. This is how you learn new tricks!) Finally, treat injuries with respect: if your body is hurt, let it heal.

BOARD MANIA

Skateboarding, land kiteboarding, mountainboarding and longboarding are some of the most exciting sports around. Here are just a few reasons why you should give these ultimate outdoor adventure sports a go!

1 Skate for free (or almost)! Boarding is a relatively low-cost hobby. All you need is a board, helmet and pads to get started. Invest in an instructor to teach you the basics in a couple of hours, and with a bit of practice and flair, you may be good enough to enter competitions before you know it!

2 Board the world! No matter where you live, you will find an urban skate park, woodland, hillside or city street with interesting obstacles and challenges waiting for you and your board.

3 Skate yourself fit! Board sports are a fantastic way to improve your balance, stamina and coordination skills. Not only will your body be healthier, your brain will get a workout too as you master awesome new challenges.

4 Go pro! If you are really good, you could turn professional and get a sponsorship deal. A sponsor will provide you with funding, which means you will be able to buy better equipment and spend more time practising your sport.

5 If you've always liked the look of water sports, but just don't like water, try boarding on land. These sports have all the buzz of water-based board sports, but they are easier to learn, the equipment is cheaper to buy and, best of all, you'll never get wet! Surf's down, land's up!

Board sports are adrenalin-inducing, adventurous and highly cool. Tap into board culture and you can find skate music, fashion, art, and a whole new philosophy on life. What are you waiting for? Grab a board and get out there!

Type 'Andy Mac tips' into www.youtube.com for some boarding inspiration!

TONY HAWK

THE SUPERSTAR SKATER

THE STATS

Name: Tony Hawk
Born: 12 May 1968
Place of birth:
California, USA
Personal Life: Married
with four children
Job: Pro skateboarder
and CEO of a huge
skating empire

ACTION KID

Even as a child, Tony was an adrenalin junkie! He challenged himself to be the best at everything, from baseball to computer games. When he discovered skateboarding at nine years old, he was hooked. Tony began entering contests and soon had a reputation for his amazing daredevil stunts.

TEEN STAR

By the age of 12, Tony's skills had earned him a sponsorship deal with Dogtown skateboards. He turned professional at 14, and by 16 he was rated the world's best skater. He also picked up the nickname Birdman because of his high-flying acrobatics. Tony spent the rest of his teens and his twenties travelling to contests and shows around the world.

SLAMMED

By the time he was 31, Tony had entered 103 pro contests, racking up an amazing 73 wins. He had the most successful competition record of any skateboarder in the world. But in the early 1990s, skateboarding fell out of fashion and Tony could no longer earn a living doing the sport he loved.

SWEET MOVES

In 1992, Tony took a risk and started his first skateboard company, Birdhouse Projects. When skateboarding soared back on to the scene in the mid-1990s, Birdhouse became world famous. Tony no longer enters contests, but still rules the skateboarding scene. In 2002, he set up the Tony Hawk Foundation (THF) to help fund public skate parks in the United States.

Career highlights

1982 turned pro

1998 won his first X Games gold medal

1998 started Hawk Clothing, his own brand of skater clothes

1999 launched first video game, *Pro Skater*

1999 became the first person to spin and land a spectacular move – the 900°!

2002 appeared in the film *Jackass: The Movie!*

Visit www.tonyhawk.com to find out more about Tony Hawk's life.

TO THE LIMIT

You pause to take in the breathtaking view. Dropping away below you is the sheer slope you are about to freeride. At the top, the only sound is the wind rushing past you. Today there are no judges or time limits. The competition is with yourself. The challenge: to conquer your fear!

DROP IN

The front wheels of your board hang over the edge. Slowly you shift your weight forwards. For a moment you hang in the air. Seconds later you are hurtling down the hillside, carried by the wheels under your feet.

NEAR MISS

As you build speed, rough terrain jerks your board and tests your balance to the max. You swerve and narrowly avoid slamming into a tree. Adrenalin surges through your veins. You have never felt so alive!

GRABBING AIR

The air rushes past your face as you spot a rock drop ahead. Your heart beats faster and your spine tingles as every muscle in your body tenses. As you hit the boulder, you pop the board into the air. You soar like a bird. It is a risk, but hours of practice kick in as you flip and turn in mid air.

THE BUZZ

Before you know it, you are back on the hillside. What seemed like hours were just seconds, but nothing matches the sense of achievement. You have pushed your board and your body to the limit. You are feeling the buzz and cannot wait for the next run.

What's the buzz?

The buzz is the natural high you feel from doing an extreme sport. It is the exhilarating feeling you get from taking on a big challenge.

For mountainboarding action, go to www.youtube.com and search for mountainboarding inside out.

THE OLLIE

The ollie is one of the first tricks that skateboarders learn. It is used for getting air and is the foundation for many boarding tricks and stunts.

You will need:

- helmet • elbow pads
- knee pads • skateboard

1

Roll along at a slow pace with your back foot on the tail of the board. Then bend your knees.

2

Push your back foot down onto the board to push the tail down. As you do so, jump so that your back foot leaves the board.

3 Drag the side of your front foot up to the nose of the board as you jump. This helps to pull the board up into the air.

At the height of your jump, press down with your front foot to level the board for landing.

4

5

Bend your knees as you land so that they take the impact of the landing.

Got it?

It's worth spending time mastering the ollie, as it makes other tricks that much easier to learn. The more you bend your knees, the higher you will pop!

SKATE STUNTS

frontside boardslide

50-50 backside

vert jumps

Type 'skateboarding vert tricks' into www.youtube.com to see some amazing stunts!

16

Most skateboarding moves can be practised anywhere, from the street to a park. But for the most spectacular tricks, skateboarders head to the vert. Here are some skateboarding bests.

FRONTSIDE BOARDSLIDE

This is a basic move to perform once a skater can pull an ollie and a 50-50 backside. The boarder skates towards a rail and ollies onto it. He lands so that the centre of the board rests on the rail, then slides backwards along it before jumping off.

50-50 BACKSIDE

To complete this trick, a skater ollies onto a ledge to land with his backside trucks on the ledge and the frontside hanging over it. He then cruises along the ledge before popping off.

VERT JUMPS

The vert is a sky-reaching vertical ramp. Skaters race to the top at speed and boost out to perform a range of awesome stunts.

BEAN PLANT

The skater lifts the nose of the board and takes the front foot off before hopping back on again. Skaters use the move to pause on the edge of the vert or when travelling over an obstacle.

CAB GRAB

A cab grab is when a skater rides backwards and then jumps into the air to perform a 360° turn. As he turns, the skater grabs the board and holds on to it during the spin.

SOMERSAULTS

Experienced skateboarders can pull off thrilling somersaults. When skating the vert, some may use the coping or wall to assist their rotation.

bean plant

cab grab

somersaults

BOARD STYLE

Each board sport requires a different type of board. Here, Radar provides some expert advice on board style...

nose

truck

deck

UP THE MOUNTAIN!

Mountainboards are larger than skateboards and have soft, inflatable wheels. Most have snowboard-style foot bindings so the rider does not lose the board when getting air. Some mountainboards have brakes to make them easier to stop when hurtling down a mountain slope!

SKATE SCENE

Most skateboard decks (see main picture) turn up at the nose and tail. This concave shape gives the skater maximum control. Skateboard wheels are made from a tough plastic that gives good traction. The top of the deck can be covered with non-slip grip tape to help the feet grip and control the board.

wheel

tail

helmet

elbow pad

knee pad

LONG AND SKINNY

Some longboards look like miniature surfboards on wheels. Others resemble long, skinny skateboards. All longboards are designed for speed. Large wheels carry the board over cracks and bumps in the road and, like all land-based boards, they have trucks that let the rider carve from side to side.

KITE RIDER

Riders new to land kiteboarding often start off on longboards or mountainboards, then upgrade to shorter, ultra-light kiteboards to do tricks. The kite is a nylon sail, joined to a control bar or handles.

PLAY SAFE!

Board sports are fast and dangerous. Here is some of the protective gear everyone should wear:
• Helmets – a vital piece of gear, whether beginner or pro!
• Knee and elbow pads prevent the most common injuries such as breaks, sprains and road rash.
• Wrist guards help cope with the stress of a fall.
• Mountainboarders often wear full body armour, padding or leathers to protect their skin in a crash.

SKATE SPEAK

Bone up on your board speak with the Radar guide.

boxes
box-shaped structures on which skaters practise moves such as grinds

grinds
moves in which the skater slides his skateboard along the edge of a wall or rail

900°
a spectacular trick that includes two and a half complete rotations (spins) in the air

carve
to take corners cleanly without skidding

heelside
the side of the board on which the skateboarder places his heels

air/big air
any gap between the wheels and the ground

flatland
a type of freestyle boarding that does not involve obstacles. Tricks are performed on a flat surface

jam
getting together with other skaters for a boarding session

backside
an approach in which the object to be used for a jump is behind the skater

freeride
non-competitive mountainboarding

land kiteboarding
a land-based board sport that involves holding a kite and harnessing wind power to move the board forwards

bail
to fall off your board or to jump off before falling to avoid injury

freestyle
a type of boarding where tricks and stunts are performed instead of racing

lid
helmet

blunt fakie
to jump and land with the back wheels on an obstacle

frontside
an approach in which the object to be used for a jump is in front of the skater

newbie
a beginner skateboarder

goofy
skating with the left foot at the back of the board

pop
to make a board 'jump' into the air during a move

rad
amazing, cool

slam
when a rider falls off
and hurts himself

tweak
to adapt an established trick

regular
skating with the left foot
at the nose of the board

stoked
feeling really happy
and confident

vert
an almost vertical ramp used
by skateboarders

road rash
cuts and scratches that a
boarder sustains due to a fall

swami
an expert skateboarder

wipeout
to fall off your board or crash
during a move

sketchy
when a move is not
performed well

GLOSSARY

adrenalin
a hormone found in the
human body that causes
the heart to beat faster

**adrenalin
junkie**
a person who is
'addicted' to exciting and
exhilarating activities

aerial
in the air

CEO
chief executive officer: the
person who runs a company

concave
bending inwards

coping
the edge of a structure such
as a ramp

**dirt track
racing**
when mountainboarders or
longboarders race on rough,
dirt tracks

downhill
when mountainboarders
and longboarders race
on a downhill course

slalom racing
a downhill race in which
competitors must pass
between poles or flags

sponsorship
the deal between a company
and an individual or team
to promote the company's
goods in exchange for money

terrain
a type of ground surface

(to) market
to show something
to people in the hope
that they will buy it

traction
the grip between a tyre and
the surface on which it travels

X Games
an extreme sports
competition held every year
in Los Angeles, USA

21

SKATER GIRL

MY STORY BY LUCY ADAMS

I used to be really into rollerskating, so when a new skate park opened near where I lived, I went to check it out. As I stood watching from the sides, a local skateboarder popped a blunt fakie. I remember thinking, first, that it was the most amazing thing I had ever seen and, second, that I needed to get a skateboard – and fast! The next day, I rushed out and bought my first board.

Soon, I became a regular at the skate park and a group of us newbie skaters all learned tricks together. I used to skate 'mini-ramp' mostly because the park had a 1-metre ramp that was just perfect for trying out new moves. Before long, we began to go out street skating, building our own ramps and boxes to pull tricks on. We spent hours practising together and trying out different stunts.

My first competition was a local event that I entered with some skateboarding friends. I can't even remember how we did, but it was really rad to be a part of it! In 2002, I started entering competitions such as the Urban Games and Board X. Then in 2003, I travelled to Australia and took part in the Globe World Cup. I got all the competitors to autograph my T-shirt – it was amazing! Since then I have entered all the girls' competitions I can – Girl Skate Jam UK is the best. Hundreds of girl skaters enter and the vibe is really cool.

Skateboarding has taken me all over the world and I've made loads of friends along the way. I've got a sponsorship deal, been featured in *Sidewalk* magazine and I've even starred in the skateboarding film *As if! And What?!* It's been a great ride so far and I hope that I can open my own skate park one day – so all you newbie skaters out there, watch this space!

Lucy Adams

RAD OR BAD?

Millions of boarders and fans worldwide believe that board sports are more than just a hobby, they can be a way of life. They argue that:

1. Board sports rank high on style points! There is a cool, 'underground' music and fashion scene to accompany the sport that fans and boarders can enjoy.
2. Doing board sports is a great way for young people to have fun and take risks without behaving in an antisocial way.
3. Boarding is mainly about competing with yourself and not against others. This allows riders to develop their style and technique at their own pace.
4. By practising board sports, individuals can be active while meeting like-minded people.
5. A boarding activity can help develop the confidence and ability to cope in all areas of life – if you can surf down a mountainside or somersault off a ramp, you can face most life challenges!

However, other people believe that board sports are not 'respectable' or are just too dangerous. They argue that:

1. Doing board tricks in public spaces could hurt pedestrians, damage kerbs and street 'furniture' or natural features such as shrubs and trees.
2. Boarding's hip and cool culture can mean that boarders resist wearing helmets or other safety gear, risking serious or even fatal injury.
3. Boarders may feel pressure to spend money on expensive skatewear and shoes, which can go out of fashion or wear out quickly.
4. A skating jam session in which large groups of skaters congregate can be noisy, disruptive or intimidating to the public or to local residents.

AGAINST

Right or wrong?

Board sports can be exhilarating and exciting. Nothing beats getting outdoors and experiencing the speed and the thrill of awesome stunts with a crowd of like-minded friends. Like all sports, boards sports need to be practised safely and with guidance.

25

THE KICKFLIP

A kickflip is an impressive starting point for many more advanced flip tricks. It starts with an ollie, but you flip the board by kicking your front foot off the heelside edge of your board.

You will need:

- helmet • elbow pads
- knee pads • skateboard

1 Place your back foot on the tail of your board as you roll along. Put the ball of your front foot just behind your front trucks.

2 Bend your knees and then pull an ollie, by sliding your front foot up the board. When you reach the nose of the board, use your front foot to flick up the heelside edge of your board.

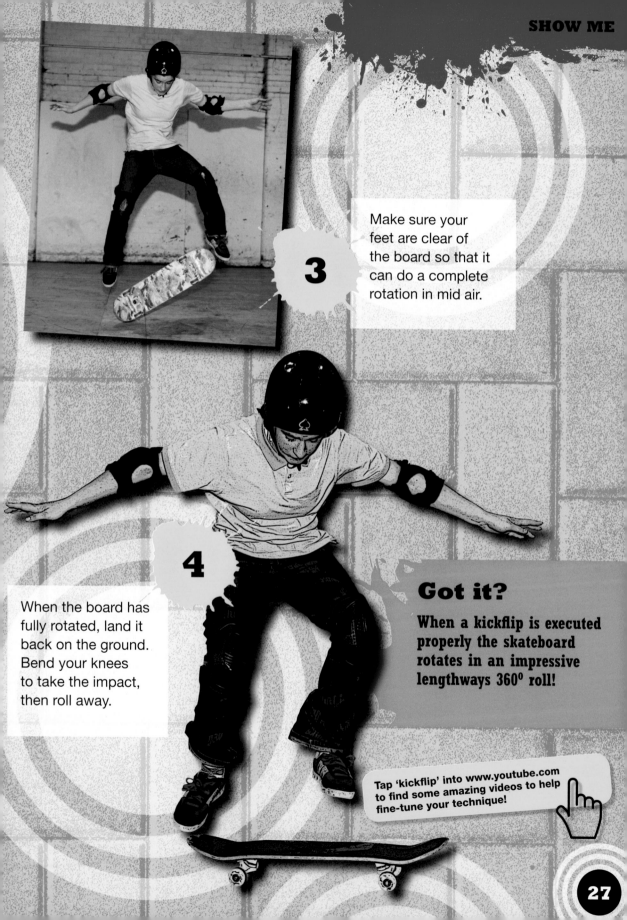

3 Make sure your feet are clear of the board so that it can do a complete rotation in mid air.

4 When the board has fully rotated, land it back on the ground. Bend your knees to take the impact, then roll away.

Got it?

When a kickflip is executed properly the skateboard rotates in an impressive lengthways 360° roll!

Tap 'kickflip' into www.youtube.com to find some amazing videos to help fine-tune your technique!

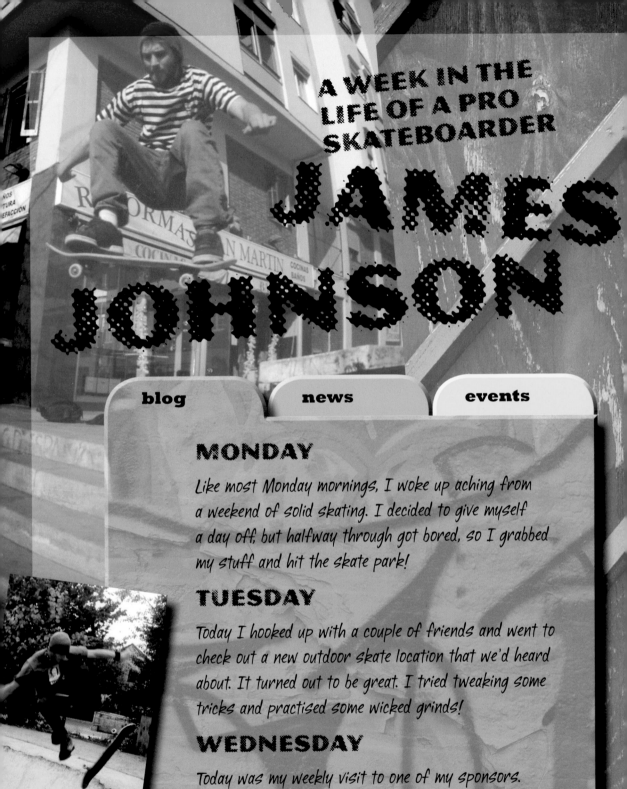

A WEEK IN THE LIFE OF A PRO SKATEBOARDER

JAMES JOHNSON

blog **news** **events**

MONDAY

Like most Monday mornings, I woke up aching from a weekend of solid skating. I decided to give myself a day off, but halfway through got bored, so I grabbed my stuff and hit the skate park!

TUESDAY

Today I hooked up with a couple of friends and went to check out a new outdoor skate location that we'd heard about. It turned out to be great. I tried tweaking some tricks and practised some wicked grinds!

WEDNESDAY

Today was my weekly visit to one of my sponsors. I went down to the warehouse to check out some new skate gear and picked out a few things, including a new board and elbow pads. I also got some stuff that the sponsor wanted me to help market.

blog   news   events

THURSDAY

I did a demo today at a local school and got paid just to show off! The kids were really enthusiastic so we gave a few skate lessons for free.

FRIDAY

Cross the word 'Armageddon' (a big battle) with 'slum' and you get Slumageddon! That's the name of this weekend's skate event – and it sums up the mix of extreme skateboarding and 'slumming it' you'll find there. I love this three-day tour – all you take is a backpack, a tent and a board. There are no 5-star hotels this weekend! The focus is on raw, fierce and fast skating.

SATURDAY

Slumageddon is filmed, then the footage is shown to a panel of judges to decide who pulled the best stunts. Today I headed out with my team of skaters to showcase our moves. We caught some awesome stunts on film and I pulled an amazing vert jump! We flaked out at the end of the day and spent the evening talking and eating by the tents.

SUNDAY

The judges watched the footage today and decided which skater was best. I didn't win, but I was still stoked to be part of it all. With the event over, it was time to head home for a rest – and a long, hot shower!

GET THIS!

130 KILOMETRES PER HOUR

The world speed record for longboarding set by Mischo Erban in 2010.

18.5 MILLION

The number of skateboarders pulling tricks worldwide.

50,000

The number of emergency visits to US hospitals caused by skateboarding each year.

12

The number of years skateboarding was banned in Norway for being dangerous!

1 MILLION

The total number of school students across the world who have learned to skateboard in P.E. lessons.

13
YEARS

The age of the youngest ever skateboarder to win a gold medal in the X Games in 2003.

2.2
MILLION

The number of followers skateboarding legend Tony Hawk has on the social networking site, Twitter.

10

The number of people who can ride on the world's largest skateboard at the same time. It is 12 times bigger than an average board!

11.18
KILOMETRES

The length of the world's longest mountainboard racecourse, at Palomar Mountain, California.

NO BUTS, GET BOARDING!

People to talk to

Kick off your boarding career and get into one of coolest extreme sports around. There are lots of organisations that can help you on your way.

Rubicon

The UK's biggest skateboard school, Rubicon hosts skate camps, events and lessons across the country. They can also bring skateboarding to your school:
www.rubiconskateboards.co.uk

Element

Find out which board sport is the one for you with one of Element's taster packages – you can choose from land kiteboarding and mountainboarding:
www.exelement.co.uk

ATBA-UK

Check out the governing body for UK mountainboarding. It runs events, competitions and training:
www.atbauk.org

DVDs, Mags & Apps

Thrasher magazine is packed with info about skate culture:
www.thrashermagazine.com

The *Berrics* app has hundreds of videos straight from the skate park.

The *Drill 1 Beginners Guide to Land Kiteboarding* DVD is packed with information about how to start land kiteboarding. Find it at:
www.amazon.com

INDEX

your mission:
To seek out more cool Radar reads...

radar

978 0 7502 6442 6

978 0 7502 6455 6

978 0 7502 6456 3

978 0 7502 6454 9

978 0 7502 6441 9

More Radar titles coming soon!

Graffiti Culture

Street Art

Cool Brands

Body Decoration

The Armed Services

The Special Forces

Undercover Operations

Police Forensics

Being a Pro Footballer

Being a DJ

Being a Stuntman

Being a Snowboarder

Being a Model

Being a Formula 1 Racing Driver

Celebrity Make-up Artist

Celebrity Fashion Stylist

Celebrity Photographer

Are you on the Radar?